HAVING BeeN IN the CITY

for Margaret,
best wishes —
and memories !

Tom

Taranis Books

© Alison Prince 1994
Published by Taranis Books
2 Hugh Miller Place,
Edinburgh EH3 5JG

Design by Alan Mason

Printed by Clydeside Press, 37 High Street, Glasgow

ISBN 1 873899 85 8

The publishers are grateful to The Scottish Arts Council for financial assistance
towards the publication of this volume.

Acknowledgements

Acknowledgements are due to the editors of the following magazines in which a number of poems contained in this publication have previously appeared: Chapman for "Weaving", "A Shred", "Fly", "Inter City", "Goldfish", "Being Afraid", "Family", "Absent-mindedness" and West Coast for three sonnets on "Women and Poetry", "Forestry", and "The Storm".

CONTENTS

On A Train

These hill-breasts
With their stone wall necklaces
Are blobbed by sheep
Like sweat-beads on a pale skin.
At Oxenholme,
Cream stone Oxenholme
Where pussy willow leans across the platform,
She gets in,
Bulky, hand-knitted, gasping
About where to change for Ely.
Her husband is silent in green tweed.
At night,
When the jumper with its agitated cables
Is laid on a chair,
Followed by the slip
And the great bra,
He lies like a cold mist
Across her hill-breasts.

Rough Sea

Old deaths are one with air and spray,
The taste of salt and the scattered sun
Glinting like fish scales
On the body of the sea.

The dead are everywhere.
They are the curled life in the gull's egg,
The rain, the leap of dolphin
Or the whale whose vast tarpaulin back
Gleams briefly through the wave.

The dead live on while anyone
Shifts to balance the sea's heave,
Watches its surge loom up,
Lean and swing under
While the next wave looms again.
The dead have known this wet skin,
And the muscles' ache, the sense
Of where the still horizon lies
Beyond these sea-hills.

I am the dead.
There is no fear of fear
In this wild sea.

Inter City

I have been travelling too long.
The bag-weight on the shoulder has become
Over-familiar, the ache
Of sleeping on strange sofas
Permanent. And now,
Just as so many times before,
The landscape runs
Outside the rain-streaked window,
Overlaid by mirrored slabs of light
And by the three red bars with rounded ends
Stencilled beside the door.

The eye seeks stillness
As a child feels for a hand
Which is in seconds torn away.
Look - cattle stand
In water that has flooded over grass,
The pools sky-white -
But they are gone.
Fairy cymbals clash
In the headphones of the man
Beside me. Lorry lights
As gold as Christmas
Follow their grey rain-road
Past secret farms
And scrap-yards piled with cars.
The telegraph-poled sky is sliced
By wires, its curds of cumulus
Rejoining all the time.

It has gone on too long, this travelling,
This making of the way past other bodies,
Riding the sliding stair, watching for lit-up signs,

NO ENTRY
NORTHERN LINE
WAY OUT TO BRITISH RAIL

After today all will be still.
The trees will not be snatched away;
Their bark, so cold, so moss-wet,
Will be there for palms to touch,
And I will breathe the air which has not passed
Through filters, cleaners, heaters
And the lungs of headphoned men.
There will be dark leaves on the path,
Rain in the wind, the smell of earth
And, like the sentence-end,
The sea.

That sweet straight line
Defines the limit of my being,
The wall of sky my cot-side.
Mother, draw up the silver sheet of water,
That I may sleep.

Home-coming

The little canyons of the beach,
Toe-deep, with blueness in the shadow side,
And seaweed like a forest seen from air
Form this geography.

In Africa, the tide-flung sand surged in,
Re-making miles of shore, a fabric
Polka-dotted with the holes of crabs.
Walk for an hour, it is the same;

But here, each water runnel speaks its name,
Not in a given word, but with its own
Identity. The basalt spur, the sea-worn stone,
The beds of mussel and rough limpet,
Every inch of it well-known.

I am illiterate in other landscape-tongues,
Misreading symbols, finding them
Too big, too brilliant,
Written in vulture-wing and fans of palm
That slap like drops of rain in the red dust.

A worm-cast writhes up, quick
From these firm ribs of water-rippled sand,
And in the pale gold of the sky
The winter sun
Which burned red-eyed in Africa
Hangs at the old hill's shoulder,
White as bone.

Having Been in the City

Having been in the city,
The straight, grey line of the sea
Brings such relief that tears come.

In the city
There is a new religion.
Concrete, the new god,
Makes urgent the old search for truth,
But in reverse,
Hunting backwards,
Seeing the skull's bulk behind the eyes
And not the sun.
Frantic for certainty,
Facts are snatched, clutched
And crumble - there is always an excuse -
In the light of further knowledge.
Mapless, hapless,
Walk concrete's worshippers,
Constructing, slab by slab,
A building in the general mind
Square against the sky.
Detailed, dove-tailed,
Reinforced with logic's steel,
Impregnable.

A gull wheels.
The boat will come across the ruffled sea
Or it will not.
Slack-jointed, heavy-limbed, unresisting,
Let the sky sweep in.
Nothing is certain,
Said the old god.
The marble card-house crumbles;

Importance blows away.
Remember how a city lay, Hiroshima,
Its concrete melted
Like frost at mid-day.
Structures are never safe.
The sky replaces them.
It fills
The lovely emptiness.

Ferry

A thin swill of water
Tips with the ship's lifting
To and fro across the deck,
Green-painted steel, not flat,
Collecting rain.
Ropes creak. The sound
Touches an almost-lost imagining
Of timber hulls, great sails,
A rapt-eyed figurehead
Below the bowsprit
And the dipping marlinspike.
No romance here.
Cars enter through the bow door
Under the ship's nose
Which sticks up in the air.
Red nose, clown's nose,
Elastic made from girders
Like Irn Bru.
A galley hand, not in a rough shirt
With sleeves rolled to brown elbows
But nylon overalled,
Coughing a bit from cigarettes and Glasgow,
Carts a black bag of rubbish to the skip.
Sit in the cafeteria. The grilles
Above the service counter rattle up
As engines quicken.
There is a smell of frying oil,
And aftershave and peas.
Assembly Stations A, B and C
Are in the lounge, the bar and cafeteria,
Where you will be instructed in the use
Of a life-jacket.
Not in the use of life.
Watch the horizon rise and gently fall.

You should remain calm.
Although we drown
In polystyrene cups and empty cans,
Sink in a sea of plastic
Where the chimera of safety
Is no life-jacket, look -
That straight, grey line remains
Calm.

Slipway

Strip down the mind.
Insert the blade,
Part and investigate.
The moving thing within
Turns a blunt muzzle to the wind
And feels it as a cataclysm
On the membrane eyes.
The body's balance
Is astonishing,
So real,
It brands with smoking pain.
Close up the wound.
Be careful.
These witnessed things
Can cut too deep,
The white-flecked sea,
The plastic bottle at the water's edge,
The slipway
Where I stand.

A Cold Spring

Small red berries
From a white-leafed tree lie trodden,
Skins split, their orange flesh laid open.
Broken twigs rot in their fluffy coats
Of grey-green moss. Clouds fly
And bare trees lean before the wind
Whose cold cuts through the bark's skin
To touch the heart.
It buffets anorak and jersey, shirt
And vest, seeking the secret human,
That strange beast which
Weaves a defence against the cold
And then, believing the fortress clothes
Impregnable,
Denies its nakedness.

Hailstones

Hailstones lodge
In the hawthorn's blackness,
Dripping, crystalline,
And then are gone,
Rising as smoke
In the winter sun.

A smoking wind
Blows over empty towns,
Containing particles
Of hawthorn, hailstone
And of human eye.

No matter.
The only tragedy
Is never to have seen.

Lines

In the water of the burn
Circles form
And form again.
The eyes of trout below the bank,
Of mouse and gull,
Curlew and mountain hare
Are round, as is the turning year.
We had hut circles,
Round houses,
Nests of stone.
We watched the moon's diminishing
And knew she would return.

But sunlight shafts
Struck through the trees
And bitter rods of rain
Were arrow-hard.
We knew that arrows need
The curved bow,
That the sea's sweet line,
Tense as a skin-strip
Stretched between the fists,
Encircles us. The men,
Belching with roasted rabbit,
Sprawled,
Argued,
Planned
And suddenly perceived.
"Look! Look here!"
We glanced across,

Round-bellied, with our children curled
Within the lap, and smiled,
For we had grain to pound
In round bowls hollowed
From the trees' kind wood
And goatskins, pregnant with their water-load,
To carry from the burn.

The men began to build,
Laying the stones
One by another, on and on,
And then abruptly turned
And turned again and once again,
Making a not-circle.
A boy
Joined thumbs and finger-tips,
Bending his knuckles,
Raising the new shape to the sun
To frame it squarely,
And then palmed his eyes,
Burned by the glare.
I watched him
On that summer day
With cold foreshadowing.

Forestry

Shut in by Sitka spruce,
The spindle tree,
Emaciated in the needle-dark,
Sheds red berries.
Pools of them
Lie among the path's grit,
Their hopefulness
Wasted like menstrual blood.
They will not be their mother's children,
The sunlight is shut out.
The path,
Man-rollered,
Will support no life.

The Storm

The storm's hysteria,
Heard in half-dream
In the window-rattling night,
Appals. The dark sky
Tears its cloud-hair,
Screams and flings wild hailstones,
Sobs in fury,
And I am afraid.

It was like this before.
Crouched in the cave,
There was guilt,
A murmuring of superstitious promises
To give no more offence
And in the morning,
A retrieval of the god-doll
From cold ash
To set it up anew
And promise, promise.

There are no ikons now,
No black-rimmed eyes
Reminding
That the world is watching us,
No sacrifice
And no redemption.
Oh God, oh weeping sky,
What have we done?

Among Trees

So long since I last stood
Here, in the ebbing of anxiety,
I had forgotten. Between trees
Is that presence which is emptiness.
It fills the shape defined
By leaves and branches. Hold the sky
Within the hands and in the mind, wait
For the dynamo to slow its turning.
Look - like the first thing in the world
A yellow leaf drifts down.

Bird Cherry

Your black-barbed interweaving
Fights for the winter air.
To witness freezes conflict,
The snapshot eye aware
Only of frost and darkness.
Your crown of thorns
Mourns the sun,
And yet you wear
Like childhood ear-rings
Hard green cherries,
On each pair
An ice-drop gleaming
In your tangled hair.

Death is not yet.
You are a celebrant,
Mingling your body's wine
With diamonds. Like the eye
Of God, a wren flits
With wings beating
At your heart.

Sycamore

Leaves
Stiff as rat-skins
Skitter into heaps
Between the stones,
To soften, coalesce
And seep down into earth
While new buds point their tips
Towards the sky.
The sycamore lives fast.

Stone-life is slow,
A moving-on of particles
Within the wash of rain,
Transferred by slug-trail
And the claws of mice
And by the hardly-present touch,
Year after year,
Of these dry leaves.

Dead Tree

The dead tree lies enfolded
In its own dead arms.
Its roots hold on to air.
Moss furs it
In a green grave-coat.
Here are no veils,
No four-square hymns,
No brave face cramped to hide
The night-time weeping.
Out of this death
The king-cup grows
And moon-white wood anemone.

Before The Funeral

What time is it?
Not many minutes gone
Since looking once before
And twice before
And many times before.
Why do I fail to understand
What time it is?
The sun shines in the dusty street.
At three o'clock
We will assemble for a ritual,
A reassurance
That time goes on.

For one of us,
It stopped.

What time is it?
I dread arriving late.
Look at the hands with care.
Note what they say.
Walk on
Until it's time.

A man sits on a chair
Outside a shop, quite still,
Black-eyed, black-suited,
With lank hair slicked down,
A mime artiste, his face
As white as piper's spats,
Acting the art of sitting on a chair.
Sticks lean aslant.
His bony hands hang slack
And time, for him, runs slow.

What time is it?
The sun, the dust, the grief,

The silver watch-hands, all
Stand still
In this
Hallucination.

Loss

She had been in my mind that day,
Friendly, open.
We knew
How things were
And how she had perceived them
In the past.
It seemed so clear
And so complete.
Not until after the telephone call
Did it seem
So terribly complete.

Funeral

"When I became a man," intones the Minister,
"I put away
Childish things."
His jowl
Is cut across by plasticised
Dog-collar hardness,
Mortified.
His welcoming
Of one more soul to Heaven
Is black-edged.
He does it well,
Having put away
Childish things.
She who lies here
In the pale wood box
Kept her childhood.
It lives on
And dances still
Over the lawns and up the sweet green hill
Where soft, small domes of daisies
Close in the ebbing sun.
This woman who is dead
Was never
Mortified.

Cremation

This funeral
Is one with other funerals,
A measured quarter-hour
Efficient
In moving mourners in
(Pretending not to look
At the white tower-chimney)
And moving mourners out
To Sheep May Safely Graze.
It takes us
On a tour of the next world
In this bus with plastic hymn sheets
And red plastic seats,
A coffin-driving engine
And one window
With no view
Through ecumenical stained glass.
We sit with downcast eyes.

It would be easier outside
To know the Holy Spirit's dance
Of love in living particles
Of air and earth and muscle
And in the heart that beats
Or beats no more.
There, in the drift of gulls,
The blaze of stars
And thrift hard-rooted in the land's edge,
Is the next world.
Inhale it with each breath.
At button-touch
The organ plays.

There,
When this is done,
I will find comfort,
Leaning
On the wind's cold arm.

Women and Poetry 1

Often, on reading what a man has said
In poetry, I am astonished by
His confidence that no-one will ask why
He wrote down figments flitting through his head
Like bubbles in the stream of consciousness.
My female caution checks such blobs of thought
And scrutinises them - and, being caught,
They burst, as bubbles will. Their emptiness
Confirms my doubt. How rash I would have been
To show such insubstantial things! And yet,
If I could cry, Oh, look, look! - and forget
My fearfulness, their lustre might be seen.
Are we too real, my sisters? Should we share
The male ability to trust the air?

Tread carefully, a child upon the hip,
A hand in yours. Beware the turning stone,
The deep gap between sedge-clumps, the wind-blown
Grasses, smooth as fur, where foot may slip
Down to a covered hole. Know your terrain,
Accept it, understand it, fit your skill
To leaf and bark and water, watch the hill
For cloud-change, find a shelter from the rain.
The men plan strategies, their eyes alight
With dreams. As sky and tree-branch interlace,
So they with us, like air in earth's embrace,
A match of equal opposites by night.
No groundlings they, their thoughts like comets fly -
But, lacking earth, they would not know the sky.

Women and Poetry 3

Sometimes they are magnificent, the men,
Flying to God with slender sticks and string
To infiltrate the heavens on frail wing
Like Icarus, who built a mad machine
Of hope and wax-held plumes, challenged the sun
And died for his conceit. They challenge still,
In folly and magnificence. They kill
Themselves and us, rather than leave undone
The do-able. And we should aim as high,
Fire poem-bullets at the public mind,
They say. But do we want to? Will we find
Contentment in this urge to do and die?
Ishtar, Osiris, Mary, pray for me,
That I may not forget simply to Be.

Now I Am Dead

So you came,
He said in the empty house.
Now I am dead,
You see the walls at which I looked,
Wanting you,
And this connection
Of your sight with dusty stairs,
Bleared windows,
Doors I meant to paint
And knives not too well washed
Jammed in the drawer that sticks
Beneath the draining board,
Brings me the pain
You always brought.
Were I alive
I would embrace you.
As it is,
I cannot weep
To see your tears.

Mourning

Now you are gone,
I think of you as fragile,
A white curl from a birch tree,
A rabbit-cry, lost
In the cold air of January.
You seemed Olympian,
Javelin-boned, raw-knuckled,
Thirteen stone.
You liked pink gin.
And yet, there was within
A quivering of baby fists,
Resisting birth
Into the happy world.
You hung on
In the amniotic fluid of despair,
And I, trying to prise open
Your tight-held misery,
Seemed an abortionist.
In that stagnant womb
Died
The little sweetness of your soul,
And now it wanders
In the winter wind.

Requiem For Renie

What has Renie done?
Left us fixed here,
Stepped away, changed her tense,
Wrapped herself in the state of being past
Like trying on a coat
Indifferently.
Never a one for mirrors,
She did not glance at sleeves and hem,
But took it.
And the coat is grand,
It gives her new importance.
Never before has Renie been
So quintessentially
Herself.

A Shred

Once the belief in human good has gone
There can be no more faith in politics.
When passion dies, it leaves the empty tricks
Revealed, the greed stripped bare. The face that shone
With fervour is historic now, a ghost
Of simple trust in coming better days.
That innocence, that unselfconscious gaze
Belongs in archive racks of Picture Post.
When cynicism rules, we dwindle through
The endless layers of doubt, and touch no ground
And wonder if belief can still be found
In anything. The barest shred is true;
That there is comfort in the sky's embrace
And in rain's kisses on the upturned face.

The Great Man
(On the intended visit of the Dalai Lama)

The great man was to come, he of the smile,
The robes, the one bare arm, he of the fame
Would come to Holy Isle with helicopters and a wealth
Of Buddhist bed-and-breakfast customers.
Wisdom, brought here like trading-beads, would buy
Both welcome and the Laura, Jim's new boat, for ferrying
The men with microphones grey-muffed against the wind
To walk the wild goat-paths, monitoring
Tibetan-Oxford words for News at Ten.

The great man was to come.
Mid-May was safe, we said, our best month,
With its sunshine and its bluebell haze, its calm.
Who could have known the wind would snarl
South-easterly, the snow bite on the skin,
The sea heave in a fury of white foam?

Goats tread their paths;
The Laura will take other customers.
The great man did not come. We could not buy
His wisdom with our awe and videos.
Perhaps he knew it was not his to sell.
Look in the hill's dark edge, he might have said,
And in its sweet conjunction with the sky.

Homesickness

This camouflage of khaki chestnut trees
Assaults the eyes and undermines the feet
With bristling piles of shell-cases. Beneath
The flodden hills, the wood-smoke elegies
Lament the dead, and white-armed skeletons
Await the fire. A panic of distress
Comes from the sky like terror. Homesickness
Sets up its maddened chant, its self-response
To liturgies of pain. No moss, no ferns,
No running out of water on the beach,
No ebbing tide where eiders bob, no stretch
Of puddled sand, no heron in the burn.
I am bereft of all stability
When robbed of that sweet line of sky and sea.

Waste

Primroses bloom outside.
Looking at them,
I eat some bakewell tart
Left over from the visitors,
Not to waste time while the kettle boils
And not to waste the tart.

But it could go to waste
Without first going through me.
I am fat enough.
And as to time -
Fill it with primroses,
Vanilla-sweet,
Paler than marzipan.
Time is not wasted
On such hunger.

Just A Thought

The sea
Would be heavy if lifted,
Hanging from God's shoulder
In a lead-grey silken length
From heaven to the waterless,
Fish-hopping
Sea bed.

Sunday Morning

The TV forecast showed
High pressure,
So the air is still.
Heat-haze blots out the hill
And renders sea and sky
Horizonless.
Gulls stand on chimney tops.
Mist thins across the white-hot sun.
Nobody moves, this sleeping Sunday morning.
Cars are unwashed and lawns unmown,
The garden dew pristine.
Does this somnambulence
Create the whorl upon the weather map?
In India, the holy man
Sits in the blazing dust
And through his calm
Allows the rain to come.
Maybe our clouds are pushed away
By rising currents of a week's pent-up
And now released
High pressure.

Fiddle Music

While the music plays
A cat
Creeps to a listener's lap,
Diving a narrow head below the hand
For stroking -
And shock numbs.
The cat is eyeless.
Nose and mouth are tabby-furred,
As is the rat-lean skull,
Devoid of cheek bones, and furred too
The empty slits for eyes.
She was born
A month after Chernobyl,
They explain.
Her mother had good litters
Normally. Four kittens, sometimes five.
But this time, just the one,
And with no eyes.

The tune begins again.
The fiddler's knee
Is bumping up and down,
Stamping the time
With bogus certainty.

The Sheuch

Below old Elsie's house
Rain makes a brown pool, prison-deep,
Marooning her. The sheuch
Cut in the bank is choked
With leaves and bramble-trail
And Double Decker wraps and mud.
With welly-toe, bulldoze the blockage,
Let the water go
To the sea and sky and wild cloud
That rains on Elsie's hill.
The circle turns. Her son will come
And bring the child.

The Old Killing House

Nothing to fear.
Armchairs, carpet,
A cat-flap in the heavy sliding door
Where beasts came in.
Flowers in a jar, stacked logs,
Warm fire, an old harmonium.
Outside, white wreckages of bone
Lie in the nettle clumps.
The burn runs deep
And brambles almost hide
The random-tumbled fridge and rusting stove.
The butcher's van hangs nose-down by a wheel,
A gutted skeleton.
Crows argue in the trees as if in hope
And yet the house is peaceful,
Sheltered by the hill
Where cows graze, and small calves
Lie curled as neat as mushrooms in the grass.

Times change.
The beasts wait elsewhere now,
White-tiled.

The Cat

The clothing of him in these softnesses
Of fur, with claws sharp as new moons
Will soon be gone.
An ugliness has come.
He is a thing
In a cardboard box,
Stuff for the grave's
Rapacious jumble-sale.
He sees me
Drive a spade through the wet grass,
And grieves for his lost self.
He is not gone,
Not yet.
I cannot comfort him.
We are both so alone.

Goldfish

Sometimes, my mother would spring-clean the fish.
The amber bowl was lifted from its place
Beside the wireless, and its mat of lace
Detached - it always clung - and in my wish
To see what happened next, I jumped about
And ran ahead to climb up on a chair
Beside the kitchen sink. And, with great care,
The bowl was tilted and the fish poured out
With all their water, through a wire-mesh sieve.
Then mother tipped the leaping orange things
Into the washing-up bowl - oh, it brings
A spasm still, seeing those quick shapes live
In water from our tap. I was aware
With magic sharpness, that I live in air.

Water-rat

A fern moves on the bank,
Making a quick, dark shape.
A water-rat?
No, just a black gap between leaves.
In the beginning, did
Illusions of this kind
Trigger conjecture in the vast Intelligence
And start the atoms groping
Towards muscle, fur and whisker
And the gleaming eye?
Miraculous,
Having seen no water-rat,
To make one out of darkness.

Fly

Carefully
Bring thumb and fingers to the fly
Which buzzes on the glass.
After the winter's sleep
She is confused,
As flustered as a big, fussed woman
Who has lost her bus pass.
She frets in my fingers,
Fizzing, but not surprised.
Nothing could be more strange
Than the hard glass with its shut-out sun.
Take her to the door
And let her go.

Vietnam Kitchen

The cook chopped lizards on a board.
They screamed. The pieces jumped.
I, afterwards, found eating hard.
Carrots put out white roots
Like nerves, and in their bag
Potatoes grew their purple-sprouting
Pregnancies.
Bread has been through the fire
To kill the yeast.
There is no purity.
The slaughtered ox is daisies,
Purple vetch, sweet grass, all dead,
Slaughtered by him.
I am the ox, the earth,
The innocent potato and the grass.
To eat is not a sin.
And yet, were I a lizard, I would wish
To die within the shade of sun-warmed rock
In silence,
With a last small, unregretful
Going out of breath.

Ostend Cafe

Fish hangs to dry in the wind,
Pegged on clothes-horse racks,
And the blue-checked cloth is clipped
To the table.
Otherwise,
The sky might fill with flying fish
And square blue clouds.

Glasgow Pub

"My daughter -
See, I love my daughter."
Yellow globes of light,
Red walls, smoke-darkened,
Empty glasses,
Half and half.
"My daughter. She's very ill.
She's only twenty-three."
Her hand explores the emptiness
Above the table.
"See my daughter, pet.
I canny cope. I'm scared."
Put on the coat.
I want to say
It's not the oozing nose
And thick-tongued words
That make me run away,
But just the pain.
I canny cope.
Go out
Into the rain.

May Queen

See me
Walking down Argyle Street,
In the sunshine,
Lunchtime
On the first of May.
Bus fumes, folk driving cars
But clouds up there
Like fat white blossoms.
I could shout,
See roses by the armful,
See my dress that flutters round my feet,
Daisies in my hair?
Who you kidding.
Underneath the railway
Is the shop, with music
And red neon
And racks of shiny ear-rings.
No pay till Friday
But I want
May morning glory,
Meadow sweetness
Blossoming.
Ah, look.
A flowered blouse,
Cotton cool as grass,
Six ninety-nine.
Too much.
But what the hell,
No lunch is slimming.
See me
Walking down Argyle Street
With a bright blue plastic bag -
May Queen.

East Anglia

The windscreen-wipers hiss,
Heaving aside great cataracts of rain,
And three white swans
Fly like ghosts in night-shirts
Towards Ely.
The sky-white road by the white canal
Hops in a flea-plague of bouncing drops
Hammering the fen land,
This black, silted, sea-bed
Where once fish swam.

Russian Cathedral

Novocherkassk. The eyes of Christ stare down,
Black-rimmed, from this vast dome. The beggars sprawl
Outside, stump-limbed. A woman in a shawl
Kneels at the icon, kisses the gold gown,
Crosses herself. A girl called Tanya stares
At candle-lit black lettering. The crowd
Of women round the priest, chanting the loud
Responses puzzles her. The harsh-sung prayers,
The incense - all this is a mystery.
In Russia, faith is new, and yet was here
As surely as the cabbages which share
The harvest altar and the history
Of hunger. As she stares up at the eyes
Of Christ, uncomprehending, Tanya cries.

Being Afraid

Black woman, how I wish I understood
The way you are. Your beauty is so strong,
It scares me. Admiration, too is wrong,
Reducing me to staring, when I would
Give all myself to know the soul of you.
I dare not. When I see your head-cloth, tied
With sureness in its balanced bulk, its dyed
Designs of black and purple-brown renew
My diffidence. I must seem ugly. Pink
And rhythmless, I have no means to show
My inner self to you, and thus to know
How you and I could start to form a link.
Maybe you feel the same. I wonder. Dear
God, what have we done to feel such fear?

Serekunda Children

You have some pen for me?
You have some pen?
They cluster round the Landrover
And stare at the tubabs'
Fat kid-meat thighs
So shamelessly exposed.
A knee is peeling.
Musa touches it,
Pulls off a wisp of skin.
The tourists laugh,
Indulgent.

Try again.
You have some pen?
Pencil?

A rosy face looks down
And eyes sky-pale, white-wrinkled,
Frown.
Now, you should be at school.

The children shrug.
There is a price
For that cool room.
You must provide
The lined white notebook.
You must have a pen.
You have some pen for me?
The pink face flushes.
You would think, it says,

With foreign aid -
I wish I'd brought more pens.

They'll only sell them, says a man.
The driver smiles
At these tubabs,
Younger than children
With their cries
That life ought to be fair.
He heard that one of them
Was jailed a month ago
For writing in the newspaper
About the unsaid things
And how dalasis go
From hand to favoured hand.
They are so brave -
So tender.
Here in Africa
Their sweet thoughts burn.
Drive on.

In dust and diesel smoke
Musa strokes
The fragment of white skin.
There were no pens.

New Moon in Africa

After the dark time, there she lies,
Nail-paring thin. Her upturned points
Hold her unseen fullness carefully.
Her symbol on the mosque lies so.
Supine, she both contains and helplessly
Submits.

Where I come from,
She stands toe-tip to stare.
She is oblique, alluding
To a truth she cannot hold.
Her hollow face looks forward
And the past is left behind
On the blind side.

In Africa, the time drifts down like dust,
Coating the earth,
And on its surface, ever-new,
We lie, as does the moon,
With points upturned,
As still and hopeful
As a beggar's hands.

Spring

Along the Hudson river in the bare park
The slush is slippery. The sleeping-still, dark
Trees this afternoon stand in a grey snow
With ice-slabs at the water's edge. I see no
Mist of green, no breaking of a fresh leaf;
Downstream, Manhattan's skyline brings the old grief
Of too much confrontation with my own kind.

In Africa, the March sun cast a hard shade
On dry-baked earth in rustling, saw-edged palm glade,
Sky-hardened. And there, too, I sensed no year's turn,
No winter's end, saw no unrolling soft fern,
No primroses. I must go home. My blood-stream
Urges a need for spring, answers a wild dream,
Even in New York's streets, where I am mole-blind.

Family

It's phone-calls mostly, now. "Oh, hello, Mum -
How are you?" Strange to think of those long years
Of Airfix kits and missing socks and tears
Of outraged protest. Like mycelium,
The family enthreaded me. It grew
As best it could, each budding shoot defined
By closeness and by what was meant as kind
Advice, so often cruel. And I, too,
Was blunted by that grasp, and could not see
That love when warped by pity forms a cage
Which traps the soul. How could the children gauge
What he and I had truly wished to be?
And yet they try. "Hi, Mum," they say. "How's things?"
I am so glad the telephone still rings.

Absent-mindedness

I am forgetting quite a lot these days.
My task-list is gap-toothed; it should run on
Like sequenced lights in a continuous phase
Of movement - but a good few bulbs have gone.

There are these sudden sleepings in my head;
I meant to buy some wine. I was to meet
That man at Johnstone station, but instead
Stood waiting outside Paisley Gilmour Street.

This, I suppose, is absent-mindedness.
Absence - an emptiness. And yet there seems
No space within my thought, and no distress
In finding duties overwhelmed by dreams.

My absent mind is filled with the delight
Of sweet horizons and the heron's flight.